Our Favorite Halloween Recipes

First Printing, June, 2008

Stir up some old-fashioned fun this Halloween. Light the house with spooky candlelight and serve homemade popcorn balls, pumpkin cookies and hot cider. Bob for apples and play pin the tail on the black cat...kids of all ages will love it!

Scaredy Cat Cupcakes

Makes 2-1/2 dozen

3 c. all-purpose flour
2 c. sugar
2 t. baking soda
1 t. salt
1/2 c. baking cocoa
2 c. water
1 c. oil
2 T. vinegar
1 t. vanilla extract

Combine all ingredients; blend well. Fill paper-lined muffin tins 1/2 full with batter; spoon one teaspoonful filling into each cupcake. Fill with remaining batter until 2/3 full; bake at 350 degrees for 30 minutes. Let cool before serving.

Filling:

8-oz. pkg. cream cheese, softened
1 egg, beaten
1/8 t. salt
1 c. semi-sweet chocolate chips

Blend cream cheese, egg and salt together until smooth and creamy; fold in chocolate chips.

Fill vintage jelly jars with candy corn and set a tealight inside each one. Their sweet glow will make the prettiest place settings!

Candy Corn Popcorn Balls

Makes about 10

8 c. popped popcorn
1 c. candy corn
1/4 c. butter
1/4 t. salt
10-oz. pkg. marshmallows

Combine popcorn and candy corn in a large bowl; set aside. Melt butter in a large saucepan over medium heat; stir in salt and marshmallows. Reduce heat to low and cook, stirring frequently, for 7 minutes or until marshmallows melt and mixture is smooth. Pour over popcorn mixture, stirring to coat. Lightly coat hands with vegetable spray and shape popcorn mixture into 4-inch balls. Wrap balls individually in cellophane, if desired.

A tasty treat for classroom parties...top chocolate-frosted cupcakes with candy pumpkins and a sprinkle of green-tinted coconut "grass."

Haunted Forest Cherry Bars

Makes 12 servings

3 21-oz. cans cherry pie filling, divided
18-1/2 oz. pkg. chocolate cake mix
1/4 c. oil
3 eggs, beaten
1/4 c. cherry-flavored brandy or cherry juice
6-oz. pkg. semi-sweet chocolate chips
Optional: whipped topping

Refrigerate 2 cans of pie filling until chilled. Using an electric mixer on medium speed, beat together remaining can of pie filling, cake mix, oil, eggs and brandy or cherry juice until well mixed. Stir in chocolate chips. Pour into a lightly greased 13"x9" baking pan. Bake at 350 degrees for 25 to 30 minutes, until toothpick tests clean; chill. Spread chilled pie filling evenly over top. Serve with whipped topping, if desired.

A vintage black lunchbox makes a clever Halloween candy holder... just fill with tasty treats for little goblins to choose from.

Spooky Cookies

Makes about 6 dozen

3 c. all-purpose flour
1/2 t. baking powder
1/2 t. baking soda
1 c. butter, softened
2 eggs, beaten
1 c. sugar
Garnish: favorite frosting

Combine flour, baking soda and baking powder; blend in butter. Add eggs and sugar; mix well. Roll dough to desired thickness on a lightly floured surface; cut into desired shapes using cookie cutters. Arrange on ungreased baking sheets; bake at 375 degrees for 8 to 10 minutes. Cool on wire racks; frost as desired.

Jack-'O-Lanterns grinning,
Shadows on a screen,
Shrieks and starts and laughter...
This is Halloween!

-Dorothy Brown Thompson

Butterscotch Haystacks

Makes 1-1/2 dozen

2 6-oz. pkgs. butterscotch chips
3-oz. can chow mein noodles
1 c. cocktail peanuts

Melt butterscotch chips in a double boiler; stir in peanuts and noodles. Remove from heat; drop by teaspoonfuls onto wax paper. Set aside to cool until firm.

Use caramel apples as festive placecards...rubber stamp a mailing tag, then tie onto the apple's stick with ribbon or raffia.

Dressed-Up Caramel Apples

Makes 6

6 apples
6 wooden craft sticks
14-oz. pkg. caramels, unwrapped
2 T. water
Garnish: chopped nuts, multicolored sprinkles, mini candy-coated chocolates

Wash and dry apples; insert sticks into stem end of apples and set aside. Combine caramels and water in a saucepan. Cook and stir over medium-low heat until caramels are completely melted. Dip apples into melted caramel until well coated; let excess drip off. Dip bottoms of apples into desired garnish. Set apples on a plate that has been covered with wax paper, then buttered. Chill for at least one hour.

Let the kids make their own treat pail...it's easy! Spray a new metal pail with metal primer and let dry. Kids can paint on any design using acrylic paints, then protect their artwork with a coat of clear sealer.

Fun Bars

Makes 1-1/2 to 2 dozen

18-1/4 oz. pkg. chocolate fudge cake mix
1/4 c. butter
1/4 c. water
1 egg, beaten
3 c. mini marshmallows
1 c. candy-coated chocolates
1/2 c. dry-roasted peanuts

Combine cake mix, butter, water and egg; mix well. Press into a greased 13"x9" baking pan; bake at 375 degrees for 20 to 22 minutes. Sprinkle with marshmallows, candy-coated chocolates and peanuts; return to oven until marshmallows melt, about 2 to 3 minutes. Cool completely; cut into bars to serve.

A fireside cookout is a terrific idea on a chilly autumn night. Join the kids for a friendly game of touch football, roasting hot dogs, making s'mores and telling ghost stories...it's all about making memories!

Fireside Mulled Cider

Makes 12 servings

3 qts. apple cider
1/2 c. apple jelly
1/4 t. nutmeg
2 4-inch by 1-inch strips orange peel
3 whole cloves
2 whole allspice
4-inch cinnamon stick
1/2-inch piece fresh ginger, peeled

Combine cider, jelly and nutmeg in a slow cooker; set aside. Place remaining ingredients in a square of doubled cheesecloth; bundle and tie with kitchen string. Place spice bag in slow cooker; cover and cook on high setting for 4 hours. Discard cheesecloth bag before serving.

A little "magic" for the kids! Put a drop of green food coloring into their milk glasses, then fill with milk as you tap the glasses with a magic wand.

Homemade Doughnuts

Makes about 4 dozen

2 c. boiling water
1/2 c. sugar
1 T. salt
2 T. shortening
2 envs. active dry yeast
2 eggs, beaten
7 c. all-purpose flour
oil for deep frying
Garnish: additional sugar

Stir water, sugar, salt and shortening together in a large mixing bowl; sprinkle yeast on top. Set aside; cool to room temperature. Blend in eggs; gradually add flour. Cover and let rise until double in bulk. Roll dough out to 1/2-inch thickness; cut with a doughnut cutter. Set aside; cover and let rise until double in bulk, about 1-1/2 hours. Deep-fry in 360-degree oil until golden; drain. Spoon sugar into a paper bag; add doughnuts and shake to coat.

Conjure up some spooky Halloween touches...stack cookies or arrange cupcakes on a black hobnail cake stand.

Orange Puff Cupcakes

Makes one dozen

1/3 c. margarine
1 c. sugar
2 eggs, beaten
1-3/4 c. all-purpose flour
1 T. baking powder
1/2 c. frozen orange juice concentrate, thawed
Optional: zest of one orange, frosting

Beat together margarine and sugar in a medium mixing bowl; add eggs. Combine flour and baking powder; add alternately with orange juice to sugar mixture. Stir in zest, if using. Fill paper-lined muffin cups 2/3 full. Bake at 375 degrees for 15 minutes. Cool and spread with frosting, if desired.

Kids will giggle when they see these! Make individual Dirt Cups wrapped in cellophane...keep each securely closed by tying with raffia and securing with a plastic spider ring!

Dirt Pudding

Makes 8 to 10 servings

1/4 c. butter, softened
8-oz. pkg. cream cheese, softened
1 c. powdered sugar
3-1/2 c. milk
2 5-1/4 oz. pkgs. instant vanilla pudding mix
12-oz. container frozen whipped topping, thawed
20-oz. pkg. chocolate sandwich cookies, crushed
Optional: gummy worms

Combine butter and cream cheese; mix until creamy. Stir in powdered sugar, milk and pudding mix; beat well. Fold in whipped topping. Layer one-third of the cookie crumbs in the bottom of a 13"x9" baking dish. Top with half of the pudding mixture, another layer of crumbs, the remaining pudding and the remaining crumbs. Refrigerate 2 hours to overnight. Garnish with gummy worms, if desired.

Wrap a plain glass hurricane lantern with vintage-style Halloween postcards copied onto sheets of vellum. Slip a tealight inside for a magical glow.

Wiggly Gummies

Makes about 2-1/2 dozen

1 c. boiling water
2 3-oz. envs. favorite-flavor sugar-free gelatin mix
2 .03-oz. envs. favorite-flavor sugar-free drink mix
3 1-oz. envs. unflavored gelatin

Combine boiling water and remaining ingredients; stir until dissolved. Pour into a lightly greased 8"x8" baking pan; cover and chill for 2 to 3 hours, until completely set. Cut into 1/4-inch strips to form "worms."

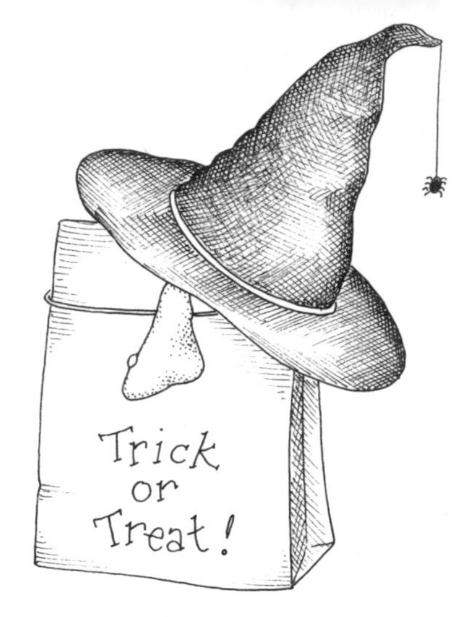

A treat and a costume all in one! Once Corny Crispy Rice Treats are wrapped and inside a brown lunch bag, fold the top down, tie on a rubber nose and top with a witch's hat.

Corny Crispy Rice Treats

Makes 1-1/2 to 2 dozen

1/2 c. butter
9 c. mini marshmallows
10 c. crispy rice cereal
1 c. candy corn
1 c. Indian candy corn
3/4 c. mini semi-sweet chocolate chips
2 drops yellow and 1 drop red food coloring
20 candy pumpkins

Melt together butter and marshmallows in a large saucepan over medium heat; stir until smooth. In a large bowl, combine cereal, candy corn and chocolate chips. Blend food coloring into marshmallow mixture, adding more coloring if necessary to reach desired shade of orange. Add marshmallow mixture to cereal mixture; stir quickly to combine. Spread in a buttered 13"x9" baking pan; press with buttered hands. While still warm, press on candy pumpkins spaced 1-1/2 to 2 inches apart. Refrigerate for one hour, or until firm; cut into squares. To make thinner treats, use a 15"x10" jelly-roll pan.

Have a Halloween film festival every weekend in October.
Check out the library or video store for old classics
or even a newer movie, then pop some popcorn
and invite friends over!

Fudge Fingers

Makes 3 dozen

4-1/2 c. sugar
14-oz. can sweetened condensed milk
1 c. butter
18-oz. pkg. semi-sweet chocolate chips
2 c. chopped nuts
1 T. vanilla extract

Bring sugar and milk to a rolling boil in a heavy saucepan; boil for 10 minutes. Remove from heat; stir in remaining ingredients until butter and chocolate chips are melted. Pour into an ungreased 13"x9" baking pan; cool to room temperature. Cut into "fingers;" store in an airtight container in the refrigerator.

Fill icing cones with homemade candies and tie with curling ribbon, then heap in a pretty basket. Guests will love choosing one as a party favor!

Buttery Maple-Walnut Drops

Makes 4 dozen

2-1/4 c. all-purpose flour
1 t. baking soda
1 t. salt
1 c. butter, softened
3/4 c. sugar
3/4 c. brown sugar, packed
1-1/2 t. maple flavoring
2 eggs, beaten
1-1/2 c. chopped walnuts

Whisk flour, baking soda and salt in a small bowl; set aside. In another bowl, beat butter, sugars and maple flavoring until creamy; beat in eggs. Gradually add flour mixture and stir in walnuts. Drop by rounded tablespoonfuls onto ungreased baking sheets, placing about 1-1/2 inches apart. Bake at 375 degrees for 9 to 11 minutes. Cool on wire racks.

Little ones will love playing spooky Tic-Tac-Toe! Just cut a board from black cardstock and divide into 9 squares using glued-in-place ribbon. Cut-outs of ghosts and pumpkins make great game pieces.

Magic No-Bake Cookies

Makes 6 to 7 dozen

4 c. sugar
1 c. margarine
1 c. milk
6 T. baking cocoa
1 c. crunchy peanut butter
6 c. quick-cooking oats, uncooked
Optional: 1 c. chopped walnuts, 1 c. sweetened flaked coconut

In a large saucepan, combine sugar, margarine, milk and cocoa; mix well. Bring to a boil over low heat; boil for one minute. Add peanut butter, stirring until melted. Add oats and, if desired, nuts or coconut. Mix well; drop by teaspoonfuls onto wax paper. Let stand until set.

Roasted pumpkin seeds are so delicious! Rinse 2 cups of seeds; dry on paper towels. Toss with one tablespoon of oil and place on an ungreased baking sheet. Bake at 350 degrees for 20 minutes; stir every 5 minutes. Remove from oven and sprinkle with salt.

Frost-on-the-Pumpkin Pie

Serves 8

1/4 c. margarine, melted
1-1/2 c. gingersnap cookies, crushed
15-oz. can pumpkin
1 pt. vanilla ice cream, softened
1 c. powdered sugar
1 t. pumpkin pie spice
8-oz. container frozen whipped topping, thawed

Stir margarine and cookie crumbs together; press into an ungreased 9" pie plate. Refrigerate. Combine pumpkin, ice cream, powdered sugar and spice; blend until smooth. Fold in whipped topping; pour into crust. Freeze for several hours; let stand at room temperature for 20 to 25 minutes before serving. Serves 8.

Fill grab bags with goodies other than candy...glow-in-the-dark rubber balls, cat or candy corn-shaped erasers, plastic spider rings, Jack-'O-Lantern yo-yos or silly spectacles.

Ghostly Whispers

Makes 3 to 4 dozen

1 c. butter, softened
1 c. sugar
1 egg, beaten
1 t. vanilla extract
1 t. almond extract
2-1/4 c. all-purpose flour
1/2 t. baking soda
1/2 t. salt
2 c. sweetened flaked coconut
Garnish: additional sugar

Blend butter and sugar; add egg and extracts. In a separate bowl, mix flour, baking soda and salt together; gradually blend into butter mixture. Fold in coconut. Drop dough by heaping tablespoonfuls onto parchment paper-lined baking sheets. Sprinkle each cookie with additional sugar; press with the bottom of a sugar-coated glass to flatten slightly. Bake at 325 degrees for 12 to 15 minutes; cool on a wire rack.

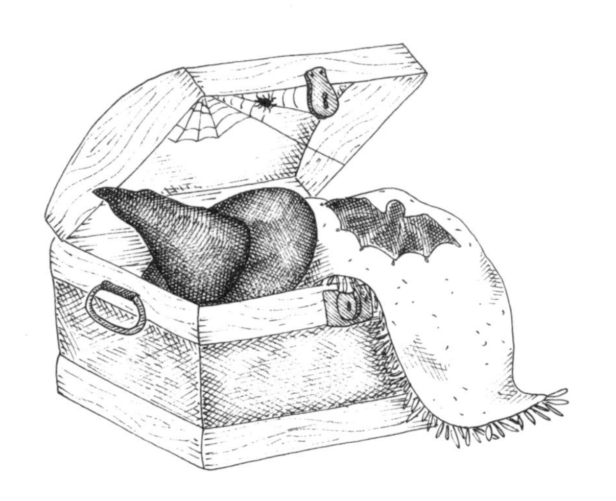

Remember the littlest trick-or-treater with a photo snapped on the big night! Frame with a mat decorated with Halloween stickers or old-fashioned candy wrappers.

Pumpkin-Chocolate Chip Cookies

Makes 3 dozen

18-1/2 oz. pkg. spice cake mix
15-oz. can pumpkin
6-oz. pkg. semi-sweet chocolate chips

Combine ingredients and mix well. Drop by teaspoonfuls onto ungreased baking sheets. Bake for 14 minutes at 375 degrees. Cool on a wire rack.

Bright yellow, red, and orange,
The leaves come down in hosts;
The trees are Indian princes,
But soon they'll turn to ghosts.

–William Allingham

Pecan Bites

Makes about 1-1/2 dozen

1 c. brown sugar, packed
1/2 c. all-purpose flour
1 c. chopped pecans
2/3 c. butter, melted and cooled
2 eggs, beaten

Combine brown sugar, flour and pecans; set aside. Blend butter and eggs together; mix into flour mixture. Fill greased and floured mini muffin tins 2/3 full; bake at 350 degrees for 22 to 25 minutes. Cool on a wire rack.

When family & friends get together for an autumn barn party, dust off an old-fashioned double wash tub and put it to work! The roomy twin tubs are ideal for filling with ice and jugs of cider or bottles of soda and water.

“Poison Apple” Bars

Makes one dozen

1/2 c. butter
1 c. sugar
1 egg, beaten
1 c. plus 1 T. all-purpose flour
1 t. cinnamon
1/2 t. baking soda
1/2 t. baking powder
1/4 t. salt
1 c. apple, cored, peeled and chopped

Mix all ingredients together in order given in an ungreased 10"x10" baking pan. Bake at 350 degrees for 40 minutes. Cool and cut into bars. Makes one dozen.

Make a pumpkin-shaped cake, it's easy! Place one Bundt® cake upside-down on a cake stand, place a second cake, right-side up on top and secure the two with frosting. Ice with orange frosting or glaze.

Fall Harvest Cake

Makes 12 servings

1-1/2 c. sugar
1/2 c. brown sugar, packed
1/2 t. salt
2 t. baking soda
2 t. cinnamon
1/4 t. nutmeg
1/4 t. ground ginger
1 c. oil
1/2 t. vanilla extract
4 eggs, beaten
2 c. all-purpose flour
15-oz. can pumpkin
1 apple, cored, peeled and chopped
1/2 c. chopped pecans
16-oz. container cream cheese frosting

Mix first 10 ingredients together; add flour, 1/2 cup at a time. Blend in pumpkin; fold in apple and pecans. Pour into a greased and floured Bundt® pan; bake at 350 degrees for 70 minutes. Cool 20 minutes in pan; turn out and complete cooling on a wire rack. Frost when cool.

Here's a bag that can be whipped up in minutes. Fill an orange paper bag with goodies, gather the top and secure with a rubber band. Hide the rubber band with green florists' tape to create a stem.

Nutty Popcorn Snack Mix

Makes 6 quarts

16 c. popped popcorn
5 c. mini pretzel twists
2 c. brown sugar, packed
1 c. margarine
1/2 c. dark corn syrup
1/2 t. salt
1/2 t. baking soda
1 t. vanilla extract
1 c. dry-roasted peanuts
2 c. candy corn or candy-coated chocolates

Combine popcorn and pretzels in a lightly buttered roasting pan; set aside. Combine brown sugar, margarine, corn syrup and salt in a heavy saucepan. Cook over medium heat for 12 to 14 minutes, stirring occasionally, until mixture comes to a full boil. Cook and stir for 4 to 6 minutes, until mixture reaches the soft-ball stage, or 234 to 243 degrees on a candy thermometer. Remove from heat; stir in baking soda and vanilla. Pour over popcorn and pretzels; sprinkle in peanuts. Stir until popcorn mixture is coated well. Bake at 200 degrees for 20 minutes; stir. Bake for an additional 25 minutes. Remove from oven; stir in candy. Immediately spoon onto wax paper; let cool. Break into pieces; store in an airtight container.

Paint the perfect spiderweb punch bowl for serving up magical potions. Wash and dry a glass punch bowl, then apply a thick layer of etching cream to the outside; let sit 5 minutes. Remove cream with water and a soft cloth. Use black glass paint to create a spiderweb on the outside of the bowl. Follow label instructions for washing.

Swampwater Punch

Makes 15 to 20 servings

12-oz. can frozen orange juice concentrate, partially thawed
1 qt. white grape juice
1-1/2 c. water
5 drops green food coloring
2-ltr. bottle lemon-lime soda
Garnish: gummy worms or frogs

Combine juices, water and food coloring in a large pitcher; chill. Arrange gummy worms or frogs in the bottom of a 5-cup ring mold. Fill mold with water; freeze until solid, 8 hours to overnight. At serving time, turn out ice ring and place in a punch bowl. Pour chilled juice mixture into punch bowl; slowly pour in soda. Serve immediately.

Bake a graveyard treat! Frost a 13"x9" cake and decorate with wafer cookies. Using gel frosting, write RIP and other spooky messages on the cookies. Top with bones (jimmies) and dirt (chocolate cookie crumbs).

Midnight Chocolate Cake

Makes 15 to 18 servings

3-1/2 oz. pkg. cook & serve chocolate pudding mix
18-1/2 oz. pkg. chocolate cake mix
12-oz. pkg. semi-sweet chocolate chips

Prepare pudding according to package directions; blend in dry cake mix. Spread in a lightly greased and floured 13"x9" baking pan; sprinkle with chocolate chips. Bake at 350 degrees for 20 to 25 minutes.

Light the way for mischievous goblins with a path of glowing pumpkins. Use cookie cutters as patterns to carve out shapes and then tuck strands of electric lights inside each. Use battery-operated lights or hide the utility cords connecting each strand with pine needles or mulch.

Peanut Butter Fudge

Makes 2 pounds

1 t. cornstarch
1 T. water
16-oz. pkg. brown sugar
3 T. sugar
1 T. butter
1/2 c. milk
1 t. vanilla extract
8-oz. jar creamy peanut butter

Mix cornstarch and water; set aside. In a heavy saucepan over medium heat, stir together sugars, butter and milk until sugars dissolve. Continue cooking until mixture reaches the soft-ball stage, or 234 to 243 degrees on a candy thermometer. Stir in cornstarch mixture; immediately remove from heat and mix well. Blend in vanilla and peanut butter. Pour into a buttered 8"x8" baking pan. Chill until set; cut into squares.

Creepy laughter, crashing thunder, rattling chains...
don't forget to pick up a CD or tape of scary sounds!

Mud Pie

Makes 8 servings

1-1/2 c. chocolate wafers, crushed
1/4 c. butter, melted
1 qt. coffee ice cream, softened
1-1/2 c. fudge ice cream topping
Garnish: whipped topping, slivered almonds

Combine wafer crumbs and butter; mix well. Press into a 9" pie plate. Spread with ice cream; place in freezer until ice cream is firm. Top with fudge sauce; freeze for 8 hours to overnight. Slice pie into 8 wedges and place on chilled dessert plates. Top each wedge with whipped topping and slivered almonds.

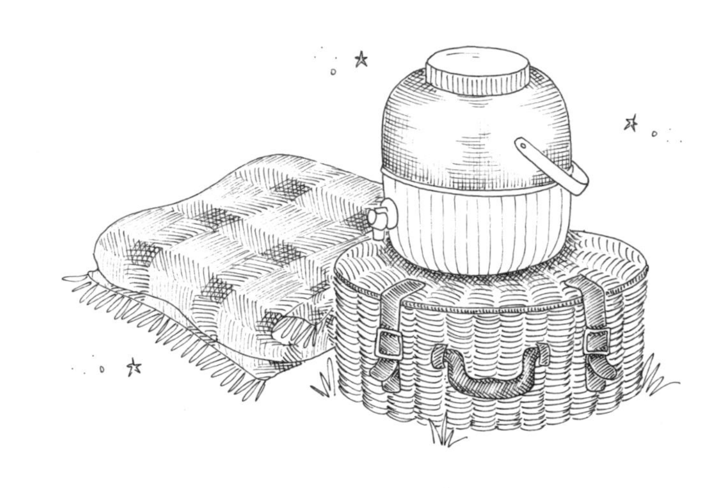

This year, tote a picnic to the pumpkin patch! Crisp air, blue skies and family...perfect for memory making.

Great Pumpkin Cheese Ball

Makes 12 servings

8-oz. pkg. cream cheese, softened
10-oz. container sharp Cheddar cold-pack cheese spread
1/4 c. crumbled blue cheese
2 t. Worcestershire sauce
1/4 t. celery salt
1/4 t. onion salt
1/2 c. walnuts, finely chopped
1 t. paprika
Garnish: 1 pretzel rod, broken in half
assorted crackers

Blend together cheeses until smooth. Stir in Worcestershire sauce, celery salt and onion salt, adding more to taste if desired. Shape into a ball and set on serving plate; cover and chill for 2 to 3 hours, until firm. Score vertical lines with a knife to resemble a pumpkin. Toss walnuts with paprika; press into surface of cheese ball. Break pretzel rod in half and insert in top for stem. Arrange crackers around cheese ball.

Drive guests batty...cut out flying bats from sheets of black adhesive shelf liner. They easily adhere to mirrors or windows and remove in a snap; just peel them right off.

Honey-Glazed Bat Wings

Makes 1-1/2 to 2 dozen

2 lbs. chicken wings
1/2 c. barbecue sauce
1/2 c. honey
1/2 c. soy sauce

Arrange chicken wings in a greased 13"x9" baking pan; set aside. Whisk remaining ingredients together; pour over wings. Bake at 350 degrees for 45 to 50 minutes, or until juices run clear when chicken is pierced with a fork.

Slip a dress and apron on your scarecrow this season and she'll be an instant hit as a scarecrone!

Rye Mini Party Pizzas

Makes 12 to 15 servings

1 lb. ground sausage
1 lb. ground beef
16-oz. pkg. pasteurized process cheese spread, cubed
1 T. catsup
1 t. Worcestershire sauce
1 to 2 loaves sliced party rye

Brown sausage and beef in a large skillet over medium-high heat; drain. Add cheese and stir over low heat until melted. Add catsup and Worcestershire sauce. Spoon meat mixture onto rye slices by tablespoonfuls; arrange on a lightly greased baking sheet. Bake at 350 degrees for 10 to 12 minutes, or until cheese bubbles and bread is crisp.

Create a spooky greeting for trick-or-treaters...it's simple! Paint a dried bottle gourd white and use a black felt tip pen to add a face. Arrange several in a straw-filled wagon.

Knucklebones

Makes about one dozen

2 T. milk
1 egg
16-oz. pkg. frozen ravioli, thawed
2/3 to 1 c. seasoned bread crumbs
oil for deep-frying
grated Parmesan cheese to taste
Garnish: spaghetti sauce

Beat milk and egg together; dip ravioli in mixture and coat with bread crumbs. Heat 1/2-inch depth oil in skillet; cook ravioli on each side until golden. Drain; sprinkle with Parmesan cheese. Serve with warm spaghetti sauce for dipping.

On Halloween, tuck tealights inside paper bag luminarias and line them up along the walk...the flickering light will lead little trick-or-treaters right to your door.

Can't-Eat-One Bacon Swirls

Makes 3 dozen

6 slices bacon, crisply cooked and crumbled
4-oz. can mushrooms, drained and chopped
1/4 c. mayonnaise
1/2 t. garlic powder
8-oz. tube refrigerated crescent rolls
2 3-oz. pkgs. cream cheese, softened
1 egg white, beaten
Garnish: poppy seed

Mix together bacon, mushrooms, mayonnaise and garlic powder; set aside. Separate crescent rolls into 4 rectangles; press together perforations. Spread rectangles with cream cheese; top with bacon mixture. Roll lengthwise; slice into one-inch pieces. Arrange on an ungreased baking sheet. Brush with egg white; sprinkle with poppy seed. Bake for 9 minutes at 375 degrees, until golden.

Dress up a mantel with a Halloween village...distress painted wooden houses with sandpaper, add some creepy "cobwebs" and toy winged creatures of all kinds...bats, owls and crows are particularly eerie.

Chili-Cheese Cauldron

Makes 9 to 10 cups

1-1/2 lbs. ground beef, browned and drained
2 10-oz. cans tomatoes with chiles
1-1/4 oz. pkg. chili seasoning mix
32-oz. pkg. pasteurized process cheese spread, cubed

Mix together ground beef, tomatoes and seasoning in a slow cooker and set aside. Place cheese in a microwave-safe bowl. Microwave on high setting for 5 to 6 minutes until melted, stirring after 3 minutes. Add cheese to ground beef mixture. Cover and cook on low setting for one to 1-1/2 hours until warmed through, stirring occasionally. Keep warm in a slow cooker.

Line up these clever candles on the mantel or dining room table. Just hollow out a few mini pumpkins and pop a tealight inside. So simple!

Mummy Hot Dogs

Makes 12 servings

11-oz. tube refrigerated bread stick dough
12 hot dogs
1 egg, beaten
1 T. water
Garnish: mustard

Separate dough into strips. Wrap one strip of dough around each hot dog, leaving 1/2 inch uncovered for "face." Arrange on a lightly greased baking sheet. Whisk together egg and water; brush over dough. Bake at 350 degrees for 14 to 16 minutes, until golden. Dot mustard on hot dogs with a toothpick to form "eyes."

Kids will giggle over the floating "hands" in their Bubblin' Berry Brew! Rinse out a pair of vinyl gloves and fill with water. Tie the ends tightly into knots and place in the freezer. When frozen, cut off the knots, remove the gloves and place in punch.

Bubblin' Berry Brew

Makes 16 servings

2 8-oz. cans frozen raspberry concentrate
12-oz. can frozen cranberry juice concentrate
12-oz. can frozen lemonade concentrate
1/4 c. lemon juice
1 c. frozen raspberries
2 12-oz. cans ginger ale
2 12-oz. cans club soda

Combine frozen concentrates and lemon juice in a large pitcher. Let stand until thawed; mix well. Add frozen raspberries without stirring; chill. At serving time, add ginger ale and soda; mix well. Serve immediately.

The rich color of vintage copper shines in the fall. Strainers, pots, molds and trays are not only practical, but filled with mums, dahlias, yarrow or bittersweet, they make decorating a snap!

Monster Eyes

Makes about 6 dozen

2 c. mayonnaise
2 c. sour cream
1 T. seasoned salt flavor enhancer
1 T. dill weed
1 onion, diced
2 2-1/2 oz. pkgs. deli corned beef, chopped
40 mini bagels, split
Garnish: black olives, halved or sliced

Mix together all ingredients except bagels and olives; chill one hour before serving. Spread about one tablespoon mixture on each bagel half; top with a black olive half or slice.

Crispy air and azure skies,
High above, a white cloud flies,
Bright as newly fallen snow.
Oh the joy to those who know October!

-Joseph Pullman Porter

Armadillo Eggs

Makes 16

16-oz. jar whole jalapeños, drained, seeded and sliced lengthwise
2 c. shredded Cheddar cheese
1 lb. ground pork sausage
2 10-oz. tubes refrigerated biscuit dough

Stuff jalapeños with cheese. Divide sausage into 16 small balls; press into thin strips. Place a stuffed jalapeño onto each sausage strip; roll jalapeño in the sausage, pressing firmly. Place wrapped jalapeños on an ungreased baking pan and bake 40 to 50 minutes at 350 degrees, until sausage is browned. Remove from oven; allow to cool 10 minutes. Flatten biscuits; wrap one jalapeño roll in each biscuit and return to pan. Bake at 350 degrees for 10 to 12 minutes, until golden.

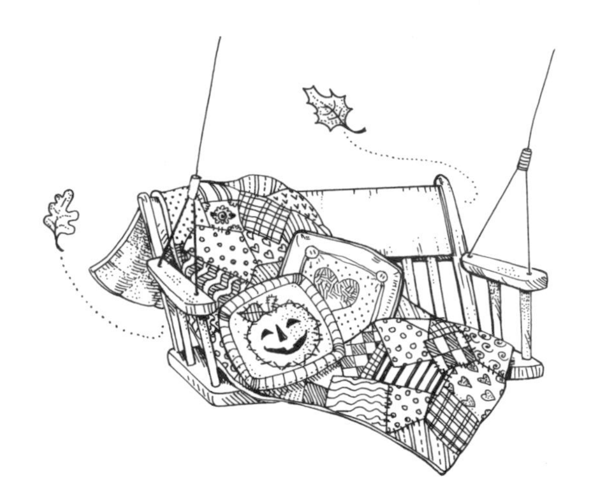

A great slumber party idea...start a ghost story circle. Sit in a circle and begin telling a scary ghost story. Each person adds to the story until it reaches a surprise ending!

Dracula's Salsa

Makes 3 to 4 cups

3 tomatoes, seeded and chopped
1 onion, chopped
3 cloves garlic, minced
1 red pepper, chopped
1 green pepper, chopped
1 jalapeño pepper, minced
1/4 c. fresh cilantro, chopped
juice of 2 limes
1/8 t. sugar
tortilla chips

Combine ingredients except tortilla chips together; mix well. Cover and refrigerate for 2 to 3 hours. Serve with tortilla chips.

Give a creepy, crawly Halloween touch to a buffet table of appetizers. There's nothing like bugs crawling up and across the tablecloth...plastic ones, that is! "Bugs" secure and remove easily with double-stick tape.

Pull-Apart Pizza Bread

Makes about 2 dozen

12-oz. tube refrigerated flaky biscuits, quartered
1 T. olive oil
12 slices pepperoni, quartered
1/4 c. shredded mozzarella cheese
1 onion, chopped
1 t. Italian seasoning
1/4 t. garlic salt
1/4 c. grated Parmesan cheese

Brush biscuits with oil; set aside. Combine remaining ingredients in a bowl; add biscuits. Toss well; arrange in a Bundt® pan lined with well-greased aluminum foil. Bake at 400 degrees for 15 minutes. Turn bread out of pan; pull apart to serve.

Create a pumpkin man to greet visitors. Stack up 3 pumpkins snowman-style, removing stems and trimming bottoms as needed so they sit flat. Add twig arms and a whimsical face...fun!

Frightfully Delicious Dip

Makes about 4 cups

14-oz. can artichoke hearts, drained and quartered
1-1/2 oz. pkg. garlic-flavored soup mix
1 c. shredded Swiss cheese
1 c. mayonnaise
1 c. sour cream

Mix all ingredients together; spread in a greased 13"x9" baking pan. Bake at 350 degrees for 30 minutes.

Place feathered faux black crows in the windows, on lampshades and all around the house for a spooky Halloween feel.

Cajun Spiced Pecans

Serves 12 to 16

16-oz. pkg. pecan halves
1/4 c. butter, melted
1 T. chili powder
1 t. dried basil
1 t. dried oregano
1 t. dried thyme
1 t. salt
1/2 t. onion powder
1/4 t. garlic powder
1/4 t. cayenne pepper

Combine all ingredients in a slow cooker. Cover and cook on high setting for 15 minutes. Turn to low setting and cook, uncovered, for 2 hours, stirring occasionally. Transfer nuts to a baking sheet; cool completely. Store in an airtight container.

An old-fashioned stoneware butter crock makes a festive fall centerpiece when filled with Indian corn and dried flowers.

Saucy Meatballs

Makes 15 servings

3 lbs. ground beef
12-oz. can evaporated milk
1 c. quick-cooking oats, uncooked
1 c. saltine crackers, crushed
2 eggs, beaten
1/2 c. onion, chopped
2 t. chili powder
1/2 t. garlic salt
2 t. salt
1/2 t. pepper

Combine all ingredients, mixing thoroughly. Shape into one-inch balls; arrange in an ungreased 13"x9" baking pan. Cover with sauce; bake at 350 degrees for one hour, basting occasionally.

Sauce:

2 c. catsup
1 c. brown sugar, packed
1/4 c. onion, chopped
1/2 t. smoke-flavored cooking sauce
1/2 t. garlic salt

Combine all ingredients; mix well.

Paint and stencil a Shaker box with primitive fall designs...choose pumpkins, stars, a checkerboard border and a crackle finish to make the box look old. Filled with homemade snack mix, this is one treat sure to be enjoyed!

Nuts & Bolts

Makes 10 cups

4 c. bite-size crispy corn cereal squares
4 c. bite-size crispy rice cereal squares
1 c. dry-roasted peanuts
1 c. mini pretzel twists
1 t. sugar
2 t. paprika
1/2 t. garlic salt
1/2 t. onion powder
1/4 t. dry mustard
1/8 t. Cajun seasoning
3 T. oil
1-1/2 t. Worcestershire sauce
1/2 t. smoke-flavored cooking sauce

Place cereal, peanuts and pretzels in a 2-gallon plastic zipping bag; set aside. Mix together sugar and spices; set aside. Combine oil and sauces; mix well and pour over cereal mixture. Close bag; toss gently until well-coated. Add spice mixture a little at a time, close bag and toss until well-coated. Store in an airtight container.

Give your fireplace a welcoming autumn glow...fill it with pots of flame-colored orange and yellow marigolds or mums.

Finger-Lickin' Ribs

Serves 8 to 10

3 to 4 lbs. baby back pork ribs
salt and pepper to taste
garlic salt to taste
8-oz. bottle Russian salad dressing
3/4 c. pineapple juice

Slice ribs into several portions to fit into slow cooker; sprinkle with salt and pepper. Arrange in a slow cooker; add enough water to just cover. Cover and cook on high setting for 6 to 7 hours, until tender; drain. Arrange ribs on a broiler pan and sprinkle with garlic salt. Combine salad dressing and pineapple juice in a small mixing bowl; brush ribs with half the sauce. Broil until browned; turn over, brush with remaining sauce and broil other side.

Make Halloween foods a little spookier! Freeze olive slices in water for eyeball ice cubes, turn pretzel dough into monster toes (add a plain almond to each for the nail!) and use cookie cutters to turn rye bread into black cat toast.

2-Headed Salad

Makes 4 servings

1 head lettuce, chopped
1 head cauliflower, chopped
1 sweet onion, chopped
1 lb. bacon, crisply cooked and crumbled
1-1/2 c. mayonnaise
1/4 c. sugar
1/3 c. grated Parmesan cheese

Layer ingredients in a bowl in order listed; cover and refrigerate overnight. Gently toss when ready to serve.

Corral kitchen utensils with a playful candy wrapper pail. Apply découpage medium to the pail with a foam brush, smooth on wrappers, and then coat the wrappers with another coat of découpage medium.

Chicken & Apple Patties

Makes 4 servings

2 T. olive oil
1 red apple, cored, peeled and chopped
1 red onion, chopped
1 lb. ground chicken
2 T. poultry seasoning

Heat olive oil in a skillet over medium heat. Sauté apple and onion until tender; cool slightly. In a large bowl, combine ground chicken, seasoning and apple mixture. Shape into 4 patties. Fry in a greased skillet over medium heat for 4 minutes per side, until golden.

Start a delicious soup supper tradition on Halloween night. The soup stays simmering hot while you hand out treats, and it isn't too filling, so everyone has more room to nibble on goodies!

Prize-Winning Chili

Makes 10 to 12 servings

1-1/2 lbs. ground beef
1 onion, chopped
1 clove garlic, minced
29-oz. can tomato sauce
28-oz. can diced tomatoes
2 cubes beef bouillon
2 1-1/4 oz. pkgs. chili seasoning mix
7-oz. can diced green chiles
16-oz. can pinto beans, drained and rinsed
16-oz. can red kidney beans, drained and rinsed
Garnish: sour cream, shredded Cheddar cheese, minced onion

Brown ground beef, onion and garlic in a skillet over medium heat; drain. Mix together remaining ingredients except garnish in a large stockpot; add ground beef mixture. Cover and cook over low for at least one hour, stirring occasionally. Top servings with sour cream, shredded cheese and minced onion.

A haunted house shouldn't look too cozy! For the best effect, empty out the rooms, drape tables with sheer chiffon, use only candlelight and fill vases with dried flowers.

Spider Pizza

Makes 4 servings

1 env. active dry yeast
1 c. warm water
1 t. sugar
1-1/2 t. salt
2 T. oil
2 c. all-purpose flour
28-oz. can crushed tomatoes
1 T. dried oregano
1 t. dried basil
2 cloves garlic, minced
1 c. shredded mozzarella cheese
6-oz. can whole black olives, drained

Dissolve yeast in very warm water, about 110 to 115 degrees; stir in sugar, salt and oil. Stir in flour; let rise for 30 to 40 minutes. Spread dough out on a greased 12" pizza pan; set aside. Combine tomatoes, oregano, basil and garlic; spread over dough. Sprinkle with cheese; set aside. To make spider bodies, slice half the olives lengthwise; arrange on the sauce mixture. Cut remaining olives in 8 lengthwise slices; arrange 4 slices on each side of each half to make a spider with legs. Bake at 450 degrees for 20 minutes.

Take a short drive into the country and go stargazing on a frosty autumn night. Late October is an especially good time to see shooting stars, but any clear night will provide a world of wonder overhead.

Hobo Dinner

Serves 4 to 6

1-1/2 lbs. ground beef
1 t. Worcestershire sauce
1/2 t. seasoned pepper
1/8 t. garlic powder
3 redskin potatoes, sliced
1 onion, sliced
3 carrots, peeled and halved
olive oil and dried parsley
to taste

Combine beef, Worcestershire sauce, pepper and garlic powder; form into 4 to 6 patties. Place each patty on an 18-inch length of aluminum foil. Divide slices of potato, onion and carrots evenly and place on each patty. Sprinkle with olive oil and parsley to taste. Wrap tightly in aluminum foil and arrange on a baking sheet; bake at 375 degrees for one hour.

For the best of the bounty, head to the pumpkin patch early! Just fill a wheelbarrow with pumpkins, squash and gourds for an oh-so-simple harvest decoration. Add some fun with white Lumina pumpkins or orange-red Cinderella pumpkins.

Easy Beef "Ghoul"ash

Makes 4 to 6 servings

1/2 c. all-purpose flour
1 T. paprika
salt and pepper to taste
1 to 2 lbs. beef chuck steak, cut in 1-inch cubes
1 T. olive oil
6-oz. can tomato paste
1-1/2 oz. pkg. onion soup mix
cooked egg noodles

Combine flour, paprika, salt and pepper in a small bowl. Dredge beef cubes in mixture; brown meat in hot oil in a skillet. Place beef in a slow cooker; top with tomato paste and onion soup mix. Add just enough water to cover meat; stir to blend. Cover and cook on low for 5 to 6 hours. Serve over egg noodles.

Dress up party cups and napkins!
Press leaf and pumpkin stickers on plain paper cups, and use rubber stamps to decorate paper napkins.

Wailing Wassail

Makes 2 quarts

4 c. unsweetened pineapple juice
12-oz. can apricot nectar
2 c. apple cider
1-1/2 c. orange juice
6-inch cinnamon stick, coarsely broken
1 t. whole cloves
4 cardamom seeds, crushed

Combine ingredients in a 3-quart saucepan; heat to boiling. Reduce heat and simmer 15 to 20 minutes; strain into serving glasses or punch bowl. Serve warm.

Give any sandwich a goblin face...the kids will love 'em! Arrange olive slices for eyes, a banana pepper nose, carrot crinkle ears and parsley hair.

Sloppy Goblins

Makes 14 to 18 servings

3 c. celery, chopped
1 c. onions, chopped
1 c. catsup
1 c. barbecue sauce
1 c. water
2 T. vinegar
2 T. Worcestershire sauce
2 T. brown sugar, packed
1 t. chili powder
1 t. salt
1 t. pepper
1/2 t. garlic powder
3 to 4-lb. boneless chuck roast
14 to 18 hamburger buns

Combine first 12 ingredients; in a slow cooker; mix well. Add roast; cover and cook on high setting 6 to 7 hours, or until tender. Remove roast; shred meat, return to slow cooker and heat through. Serve on hamburger buns.

Make a fun porch sign for Halloween...stencil a saying like "Best Witches" or "Sit for a Spell" on an old plank.

Velvety-Smooth Pumpkin Soup

Makes 6 servings

1/4 c. butter
1 onion, chopped
1 T. brown sugar, packed
14-1/2 oz. can chicken broth
1/2 c. water
15-oz. can pumpkin
12-oz. can evaporated milk
1 t. garlic salt
1/4 t. cinnamon
salt and pepper to taste

Melt butter in a saucepan over medium heat. Add onion and brown sugar; cook until onion is transparent. Add broth and water; bring to a boil. Reduce heat to a simmer and stir in remaining ingredients; blend well. Simmer until soup is heated through; do not allow to boil.

A dandy placecard how-to...preserve dried leaves by ironing between 2 sheets of wax paper under a tea towel. When cool, trim around the leaves and write guests' names on with metallic ink.

Crunchy Apple-Pear Salad

Makes 6 servings

2 apples, cored and cubed
2 pears, cored and thinly sliced
1 T. lemon juice
2 heads butter lettuce, torn into bite-size pieces
1/2 c. crumbled gorgonzola cheese
1/2 c. chopped walnuts, toasted

Toss apples and pears with lemon juice; drain. Arrange lettuce on 6 salad plates; top with apples, pears and gorgonzola cheese. Drizzle salad with dressing; sprinkle with walnuts. Serve immediately.

Dressing:

1 c. oil
6 T. cider vinegar
1/2 c. sugar
1 t. celery seed
1/2 t. salt
1/4 t. pepper

Combine ingredients in a jar with a tight-fitting lid; cover. Shake well until dressing is blended and sugar dissolves. Keep refrigerated.

Send friends home with a funny-faced scarecrow potholder.
Made from fabric snippets and buttons, he's quick to stitch up.

Chicken En-Chill-ada Casserole

Serves 10 to 12

10-3/4 oz. can cream of chicken soup
1 c. milk
3 c. chicken, cooked and chopped
2 4-oz. cans diced green chiles, drained
1/3 c. onion, chopped
6 c. tortilla chips, coarsely crushed and divided
2 c. shredded Monterey Jack cheese, divided

Stir soup and milk together until creamy; spoon just enough into an ungreased 3-quart casserole dish to coat the bottom. Add chicken, chiles and onion. Sprinkle 3 cups chips and half the cheese on top; layer with remaining chips. Spread on remaining sauce; top with cheese. Bake at 350 degrees for 20 minutes, until hot and bubbly.

Serve a bowl of soup that stares back! Scoop the centers from mini mozzarella balls, fill with sliced pimento-stuffed olives and float in any favorite soup...it's eye-popping!

Ghostly White Chili

Serves 16 to 20

6 15-1/2 oz. cans Great Northern beans, drained and rinsed
3 5-oz. cans chicken, drained
6 c. chicken broth
3 c. shredded Monterey Jack cheese
2 4-oz. cans diced green chiles
12-oz. container sour cream
1 T. olive oil
2 t. ground cumin
1 t. garlic powder
1-1/2 t. dried oregano
1/4 t. white pepper
Optional: 2 onions, chopped

Combine all ingredients in a large stockpot. Simmer for 20 minutes until heated through.

A grandmother pretends she doesn't know
who you are on Halloween.

- Erma Bombeck

Squirmy Salad

Makes 10 to 12 servings

16-oz. pkg. spaghetti, prepared
2 tomatoes, diced
1 green pepper, diced
1 onion, diced
1 cucumber, peeled and diced
16-oz. bottle creamy Italian salad dressing
2-3/4 oz. jar salad seasoning

Mix all ingredients together in a large serving bowl; refrigerate overnight.

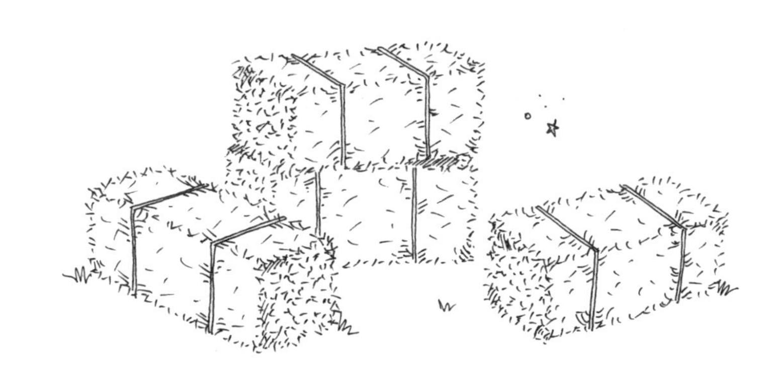

Create your own hay maze...it's simple. Stack bales of hay or straw and make a little path that runs through them. The kids will laugh all the way through it!

Sneaky Snakes

Makes 6 servings

1/3 c. sour cream
1/3 c. thick and chunky salsa
6 bread sticks, halved lengthwise
8 slices American cheese, each cut into 3 strips

Garnish: chopped black olives, softened cream cheese, sliced red pepper or pimiento, sliced stuffed green olives, shredded lettuce

Combine sour cream and salsa in a small bowl; spread over cut sides of each bread stick. Place 4 strips cheese onto bottom half of each bread stick; cover with top half. To decorate each snake sandwich, attach 2 pieces chopped black olive to one end of top of sandwich with dots of cream cheese for "eyes." Cut a piece of red pepper into tongue shape; place it between bread stick halves. Attach slices of green olives to the top of sandwich with dot of cream cheese for snakeskin design. Place shredded lettuce onto platter. Set sandwiches onto lettuce and serve immediately.

For an autumn centerpiece...pile Jack-be-Little and
Baby Boo pumpkins along with acorn and dumpling squash on
a cake stand. Simple yet so eye-catching.

Slow-Cooked Pork Tacos

Serves 4

1 onion, chopped
1 green pepper, chopped
1-1/2 lbs. boneless pork loin chops
3/4 c. orange juice
juice of one lime
1/2 c. fresh cilantro, chopped
1 T. garlic, chopped
1 t. chili powder
salt and pepper to taste
3/4 c. salsa
8 8-inch flour tortillas, warmed
Garnish: lettuce, tomato, sour cream, salsa

Place onion and pepper into a slow cooker; add pork. Mix together juices, seasonings and salsa; pour over meat. Cover and cook on low setting for 4 to 6 hours, until meat is very tender. Drain excess liquid; shred meat with a fork. Spoon into warmed tortillas and add taco toppings of your choice.

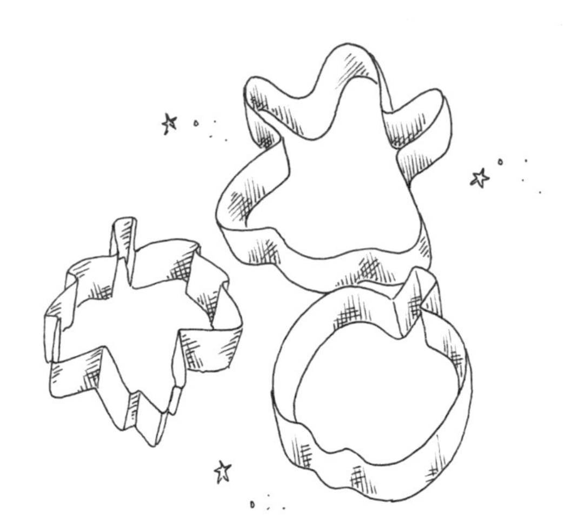

Use cookie cutters in leaf, pumpkin or ghost shapes to cut out biscuit dough...a dinnertime surprise!

Spiderweb Soup

Makes 6 to 8 servings

1 c. red onion, chopped
1 red pepper, chopped
2 cloves garlic, minced
2 boneless, skinless chicken breasts
1 T. oil
7 c. chicken broth
9-oz. pkg. frozen corn, thawed
1 t. ground cumin
2 c. tortilla chips, lightly crushed
1 c. shredded Cheddar cheese
Garnish: sour cream, dried cilantro

In a soup pot over medium heat, sauté onion, pepper, garlic and chicken in oil for 7 to 8 minutes. Remove chicken. Pour in broth; bring to a simmer. Add corn and cumin; cook for 10 minutes. Shred chicken; stir into soup. Place some chips in each bowl; ladle soup over chips. Sprinkle with cheese; stir. Garnish with sour cream drizzled to form "webs" and sprinkle with cilantro.

If the weather's beautiful, consider hosting a potluck dinner outside in all of autumn's glory! Set up a farm table scattered with leaves and a wheat-filled sap bucket centerpiece...celebrate!

Devilishly Delightful Spaghetti

Makes 6 servings

1 lb. ground beef, browned and drained
1-1/4 oz. pkg. spaghetti sauce mix
2 T. onion, minced
1 T. garlic, minced
8-oz. can tomato sauce
4-1/2 c. tomato juice
4-oz. can mushroom stems and pieces
8-oz. pkg. spaghetti, uncooked
salt and pepper to taste

Combine all ingredients except noodles in a slow cooker. Cover and cook on low setting for 6 to 8 hours. Add half of the spaghetti, coarsely broken, reserving remaining spaghetti for another use. Turn on high setting and cook until spaghetti is tender, about one hour. Sprinkle with salt and pepper.

INDEX

APPETIZERS

BEVERAGES

COOKIES & CANDY

DESSERTS

INDEX

How did Goosebery Patch Get Started?

Gooseberry Patch started in 1984 one day over the backyard fence in Delaware, Ohio. We were next-door neighbors who shared a love of collecting antiques, gardening and country decorating. Though neither of us had any experience (Jo Ann was a first-grade school teacher and Vickie, a flight attendant & legal secretary), we decided to try our hands at the mail-order business. Since we both had young children, this was perfect for us. We could work from our kitchen tables and keep an eye on the kids too! As our children grew, so did our "little" business. We moved into our own building in the country and filled the shelves to the brim with kitchenware, gourmet goodies, enamelware, mixing bowls and our very own line of cookbooks, calendars and organizers. We're so glad you're a part of our **Gooseberry Patch** family!

For a FREE copy of our **Gooseberry Patch** catalog, write us, call us or visit us online at:

Gooseberry Patch
600 London Rd.
P.O. Box 190
Delaware, OH 43015

1·800·854·6673
www.gooseberrypatch.com